TYPES IN A FRAME

introspective self-report

SARA PANTIC

ISBN: 9798609938107

Verba volant, scripta manent.

CONTENTS

ACKNOWLEDGMENTS

Many people made significant contributions to this work.
My gratitude is endless.

INTRODUCTION

I'd like to show any fellow readers of this book many thoughts and feelings that have been on my mind for a long time. Some conclusions I came to were hard to come by because experiences with people often open up new horizons. This is a pattern, one which tirelessly repeats itself. Still, when it comes to certain things, I feel safe to express my ideas and insights, and I think it's not too early to do that. When someone is so focused on people throughout his or her life and has had experiences that have left such a person burned and scarred, he or she will have two options: to live with contempt and pain or to learn to rationalize what is seen with as much as persistence as one can muster. Personally, I am still struggling with this; however I am proud when I gain victory over my own flaws.

I have an insatiable need to tell you about euphemisms in typology, ie. about things you will often come across when you meet certain types. Behind the beautified, ornate walls of a personality are quite ordinary rooms. Sometimes they are dirty or unfinished, unventilated, sometimes there is nothing, and sometimes you find quite unexpected things. Suffice to say that we are all unique yet very similar, and behind every person is a story.

I'll tell you what I've thought about the most ever since I have come to know myself, that involving our relationship with our own caregivers. We were all babies. All of us were blank sheets of paper with virtually no blueprints or ink stained into our memory, and no images shaped or molded us to be anything other than what we were – an open canvas – an uncrafted sculpture of perfection.

During that time, those responsible for our well-being, namely our own caregivers, imprinted onto us what they wanted. We did not inherit only their eyes, their noses, and their toes, we also received some other key things of which were the cornerstones of what we built ourselves into. Of course, such a thing is inevitable and most do it out of good nature, repeating the writings and scrolls of concepts, behaviors, and beliefs they too were prescribed with shortly after birth. Yet even that is only the surface, for the image is far more complex than solely ideas and concepts passed down to it, as even the behaviors and ways in which it was raised, it's needs, and it's own experiences and reactions to those matters influencing it will affect the overall portrait. For it will craft itself in such a way that it forms it's own identity and behaviors. The image sees and interprets information through a behavioral processing lense, comparatively 8 functions in typology terms.

I will first express my opinion on the compatibility of types. Types are handy to look at as puzzles. One fits perfectly into the other and together they form a whole, giving completeness to the image. But there is no such thing as ideal compatibility because certainly, the types viewed individually cannot be considered ideal. We are looking at the best possible compatibility (therefore, not "ideal") with its flaws. We will come to understand why the proverb "watch what you want - maybe it will come true" as well as the saying "beauty is in the eye of the beholder" applies in regards to these circumstances. Allow me to also mention that each type has a tendency for particular pathologies. I'll be sure mentioning that more closely in detail as well.

TYPES IN A FRAME

MY STORY

I was born in Serbia, Novi Sad, in the year 1993. There was a large war in the country where I was born. Hyperinflation prevailed. The leader of the state was sovereign and did not "catch on to the train" so to speak of world changes. He did not know the outcome of his own decisions for the future. In a world of globalism, the government in my country forgot about its obligations to international financial institutions: the World Bank and the International Monetary Fund. The financial system in the country collapsed. In addition to a bloody war, hyperinflation is one of the most tragic experiences of the recent past.

One kilogram of flour cost RSD 17,930,000 and a kilogram of salt cost RSD 87,220,000.

A pound of laundry soap – RSD 52 598 000. In that year, I was born at the center of global hyperinflation, when prices were rising hour by hour. Everything you could find in the store was bought for worthless money. By the end of 1993, bread cost 4 billion dinars and milk cost 9.5 billion dinars. The average wage was 10 DM and little could be bought. One German mark on the black market was worth 1 billion and became the only means of payment. Thirty-three of 500,000 billion notes have been put into currency. Production stopped because it was the first year since the country broke up. Along with the war came economic isolation. The Great Powers have played with us like many times before in history. Some nations will always break their spears, unfortunately… In economic history, this inflation was recorded as the longest, lasting 24 months. Prices rose 313 million percent in January. That January, I was two months old. To make matters worse, my mother couldn't breastfeed me. She was only 21 at the time and from this point of view, I don't think she had enough knowledge nor the ability to deal with problems and simultaneously take good care of her newborn baby. She was very dependent on her mother's opinion. Both my mother and my grandmother are ESFJs (2w1). My mom took me into her arms one day with the intention of feeding me. She thought she was feeding her baby because it looked like that. I sucked and was calm as long as Mom was by my side. When mom put me to bed, I would cry hysterically. The same thing was repeated for several days. It was not clear to Mom what she was doing wrong until Grandma began to convince her that "the baby is hungry". Fear overwhelmed the both of them by the thought of it.

My father was on the battlefield in Bosnia and Herzegovina at the time. He was a soldier who defended Herzegovina, where he came from and where he lived until the war. When the war began, his life changed radically, which was extremely difficult for him. He is an ISFJ (6w5). He visited my mom and me occasionally, and I can't imagine how traumatic his departures were. For mom - because she didn't know if he would come back alive, and for him – I was the first and long-awaited child - would he ever see me again? My father had me at the age of 40, a very late age to harbor a firstborn. He waited a long time on that… I am not sure because he never talks about that, but I suspect it was probably because his first wife couldn't have any children of her own.

My parents rarely talk about this period in my presence. Not at all. Everything I know today has been revealed to me by my grandmother, though I have a fear of asking her because I am afraid to hear something that would kill me inside. Sometimes, it's hard to stand the truth. It's easier to avoid things and live without knowing. My grandmother once told me that Dad fought with my picture in his pocket. It gave him strength. Tears come to me every time I think of it.

Dad was with us right then, not on the front, when it was speculated on why Sara was crying all the time. Although Dad is an intelligent and highly educated person, he was not skilled with babies. Grandma was persistent with her theory. In that place where no one looks at their own jobs, many people have come to give their opinions. None of them, in my humble opinion, can boast of intelligence and education. Fortunately, one of my mother's cousins, who was a doctor of the place, confirmed grandmother's thesis that my cry was actually crying of a hungry baby.

It was very difficult to get baby food at the time. Or so I should say, it was almost impossible. The only luck in the tragic accident is that my mother's family had a cow. They made the decision to feed me with cow's milk because they had almost no choice, and the situation was very alarming. Dad was very worried because there is no greater defeat for someone who is an ISFJ than to not be able to feed his or her child, and he was heartbroken that he did not have the ability to specifically help. He became obsessed and went to observe how and in what conditions the cow was milked, whether everything was clean and other similar things.

Protein in cow's milk can be extremely dangerous because they are not decomposed and can cause an allergic reaction. That's what happened to me, unfortunately. My skin looked withered and frightening for those around me. I guess I also suffered a lot of pain in those days. Fortunately, I don't remember the feeling, but the marks remain forever. My skin remembers, and my heart remembers. Traumas remain for life.

Dad did everything he could to get adequate baby food from Germany. It certainly wasn't easy then and I feel immense gratitude for his tremendous care and hard work.

I am very emotionally attached to my father. Today when I think about it, when I connect all the dots, I think there is something pathological about it. I managed to "get out of my grandmother" some other truths from the past.

Various people lived in that area and were quite aware of each other. The spirit of communism was very pronounced there. It should be understood that although a person approaches an individual to help, he does not necessarily always have good intentions. Often, as a small child, I was condemned to people who loved to complain. They fed themselves by telling tragic stories that had no other alternative. So I was forced to listen at the age of two about my own father being somewhere in the war and how I was without him. Because of such woeful people, I hated the sense of community, even though I spent my first years of life (the crucial years for child development) in such an atmosphere. It all influenced what I am today. A person with a dominant Fe (sense of community) but also a defiant individual (Enneagram 4).

Every time when Dad would come back, I would scream and run to hug him. Who knows what kind of thoughts and experiences of my dad I held back then?

In 1995, my sister was born and my already weak relationship with our mother became even worse. Mom and I have always been a long way from calling each other close. She was distant towards me, and my dad was often not around for us because of his work. For me, in the eyes of a little girl, I was alone in the world. I thought that was the way things should be. Many people were around me all the time, but I always felt like I was alone. Maybe that's how Fe doms make you feel… Or maybe it's about that place. I loved it and I hated it at the same time.

When Dad came home from hell, his mother died the same year. He had already suffered enough, and by then it seemed he was experiencing only accidents after accidents. His life became a tragedy. The consequences were visible in the pictures from that era. Dad looked icy and chronically sad at each. He is one anguished soul. Such a beautiful man with a wide smile and sad eyes.

My sister, as a younger child and more interesting to ESFJ women, received absolute attention. I had given up on ESFJs in my life. I wanted Dad's attention. Dad…. An iceberg, in which half of his heart was dead from an unbearable past. The brightest spot of my childhood was my ESFP aunt, my mother's birth sister, who was different from most women I was sentenced to deal with and be around there (mostly unhealthy forms of ESFJ and INFJ women).

INFJ women were relatives on Dad's side. One of them did not like children and looked at me with contempt, while the other had a tragic fate (she was in the concentration camp during the war) and I'm quite sure she was not stable. My mother's cousin, the doctor, often warned my mom not to leave me alone with this woman. I'll never know if she obeyed her. I hope she did…

From my mom's side, they were all ESFJ women. Not one of them I consider a good person. It sounds judgmental, but I realized that is the final feeling I am left with after all this time.

My mom's aunt, as far as I know, had some problems with my grandmother at a young age. That woman always tried to make her and her offspring "golden". My grandmother and her offspring were to be marginalized and always viewed from a high position. Nothing hurts me more than that. Such a concept triggers in me inferior feelings.

Now I know these things, but when I was four years old, I was taught that all the people I was around were wonderful and that we were all "one union". I really believed in that. That was my mindset. Life is beautiful. People are lovely.

Why is my dad a hero? Because he struggled to create something from zero, out of nothing, all the while completely alone after the war. He is a hero because he took me, my mom, and my baby sister out of that dark place. I still feel guilty when I talk about my childhood environment with such contempt, as if it was something bad... It is hard to discern what my true feelings about that place and those years are and what was just acceptable to feel and think back then. I was just a kid...

We moved to another country. Dad got a good job because he was well educated. By that time, he also managed to acquire the apartment we lived in. It was very difficult for my mother to endure moving to another country and to be away from her mother and all those people she was used to be around. Mom used to get all these people involved in her life, and for her, life with just the three of us was loneliness. Her feelings affected me and my sister. We experienced Mom's emotion as our own.

I remember when Mom wrote a letter to the people there, and she wanted us to be involved. I was four years old then. Those are some of my first memories. I think I cried for all these people because my mom cried. I believed I missed them. If you were to ask my heart now, I think I only missed my aunt a little, but for me, life was just getting started. I had a sister to play with every day and I had privacy. My little soul cried for it's own space and peace. I wasn't blessed with such a privilege in that place. Everyone entered the house without knocking on the door. A very strange custom indeed. It was distressing for me. As far as I know, it was distressing for Dad too.

Now I am aware of how much my dad despised it. Everything was a little bit tiring for him. I respect him because he was doing things and he never said a word against anyone. He didn't teach me to hate, not even towards those he fought against. Dad is a gentleman. He is a great man, though I don't know if I idealize him because of the circumstances I was in or whether my dad deserved this, and perhaps much more…

Although I "got rid of" that ambiance, my anguish did not go away. Life with me was easy for everyone except for myself. I think I was extremely neglected and much was expected of me. Mom and I were still far apart and I couldn't always count on Dad to be there for me. When I was a baby, I was missing very basic yet essential needs for life (food and closeness to my mother), and when I was a little bigger, all those material things had settled, and what I missed was understanding. That was all I needed. Okay, maybe a little bit of support, too. With that in mind, I turned to my vivacious imagination and my optimism. I was introspective and creative. Music was my best friend. I often knew to spend the day dancing in front of a glass closet. I had no real, big mirror, but what I had worked for me.

I felt alone but also self-centered in my ways. I loved people, however I didn't trust anyone completely. Creativity was my therapy. It was in that way I came to reduce my fears. I made my own theater and radio broadcast when I was around 10 and I forced my sister and my friends to do that with me. Unfortunately, they weren't as enthusiastic about it as I was, and that made me feel awkward. As a kid, I believed that everyone had a need to express his or herself through creativity. For that reason, I bet I was annoying for many of my friends, but I feel like their parents liked me. I was a real doer of things. The potential was everywhere. I hope I never lose that mindset! My favorite memories were the reactions of other people when I created something that truly moved them.

In those years, we only had a couple of channels on TV and oftentimes when I was left unattended by my mom and dad, I watched content inappropriate for my age. I remember how fascinated I was with a series about children without parental care. This social topic hadn't shocked me at all. I was already analyzing these characters and experiencing them very intensely. One actor was really likable. I think that the actor is an ISFP. In fact, I'm sure it is. It is interesting to watch that series at this age. It's a bit different but it's still beautiful.

The logical sequence of events that follows was that my puberty was tumultuous, and because of a lack of adequate understanding in the home, I sought understanding elsewhere. Though I was never a weakling, (Quite the contrary in fact. I was an excellent student and popular at school) on several occasions I was a victim of peer violence. Because of one of those instances, I was left with serious psychological consequences. I can say for sure that the culprit was a sociopath. Regardless of my knowledge about people and their intentions, my weaknesses are often bigger than my judgement, and I give my energy away to the wrong people. That girl was an unhealthy version of an ENTP person - a sociopath who was not independent. If I could describe it with a simple phrase, it would be to feel as if you were giving blood to someone, and that person's way of obtaining your blood was to bite you and suck every liter from your body until not a drop was left for you, and to continue sucking desperately while demanding more and berating you for not having enough, despite the fact that they have left you with nothing. So you are left with nothing but wreathing in immense pain.

I often feel like not even thinking about these people. Now, when I have recovered and forgiven them in my soul, I feel relief and I have freedom. I don't want to remember those girls... But I do I forgive them!

Things are not black. They are not white either. My whole life is made of beautiful and ugly events, as is the case with everyone else, but if I put my childhood on a scale, suffice to say I experienced it more as an overall torment rather than a carefree period. Yet that notion also changes in spite of my current mood. Introspection is not easy. Conclusions can be false from time to time. What is important is that I am now shaped by all of my troubles, ready for life's many challenges. I am more cautious and wise than I used to be. I am ready to fight and protect myself, I am ready to explain the truth to myself … Causes, motives, goals, behavior of people…

My heart is free because my head does not remember well. Such a free heart does not have the strength to spend it on returning kicks, but to steer away from its losses, forgive, and to escape the clutches of the past forever. Let everyone bear their cross. Life is much too short to be wasted. I would tell everyone today to care about his or herself with a much ferocity as possible. The One above, who is bigger than all of us, is love, truth, and justice. Living honorably and not upsetting another and sometimes giving and not seeking in return is what makes me a person I can be proud of. Creating something better than myself is my therapy and my drive. People. That's my preoccupation. It comes naturally, by default. People and everything that makes them human and inhuman is what will forever make me curious and also proud when I come to new insights and perspectives.

It was not me who chose that path. That path chose me. I don't have another one. This path is my "traveling house". It is the path without end... Colorful and wide.

That path is the ocean. One can always swim deeper, encountering some new phenomena and species, but also encounter being preyed upon and other dangers that lurk in the abyss. Swimming in that ocean does not stop. It has no end, and it encompasses all that I am. That's where I breathe.

I will convey to you what I have seen in those depths. Some things are harder to describe, but if one has a need to express oneself and has someone to listen, there is no obstacle. I will simplify things and try to stay authentic and consistent with my insights. I will try to summarize my painful abstractions in the most rational essence as possible.

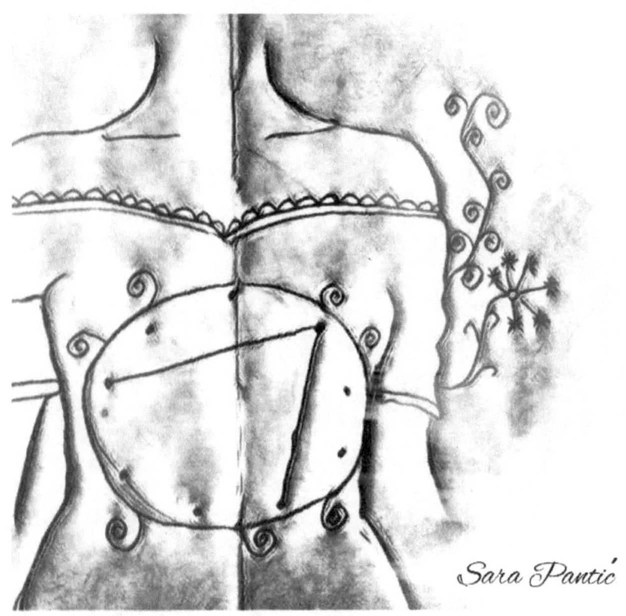
Sara Pantić

EUPHEMISMS IN TYPOLOGY

Anyone who has encountered typology on the internet for the first time was usually fascinated by the "adequate descriptions" of his personality. Many articles are written to "caress our eyes" and our ego. A euphemism is a stylistic element by which expressions that have an unpleasant connotation can be made comfortable, receptive. In life, we often use them in our daily communication with people so as not to create unnecessary conflict or to be a person with manners. So, in life, we can find sentences like:

"He went to the eternal hunting grounds." –when we want to say "He died forever."

We use the terms:

"Developing countries" - instead of "underdeveloped countries"

"Controversial businessman" - instead of "criminal" etc.

We also encounter antonomasias, stylistic elements in which the name is replaced by epithet or expression. So "fantastic four" for the Beatles, the "king of pop" for Michael Jackson, the "steel lady" for Margaret Thatcher, etc.

We often can find periphrases as well. Periphrasis is a

stylistic element that is used when we want to not name a term directly but explain it descriptively using some of its characteristics that make it recognizable. Periphrasis is every definition and surrounding expression. So instead of the word "prostitution", we will use a phrase composed of several words "the oldest craft in the world". Instead of the word "lion", we will say "king of the jungle".

In contrast to this, in everyday conversation, we also use dysphemisms.

They show the word in an uglier way. Instead of saying "she died", by using dysphemism, the sentence would take the form "she became food for the worms".

Litotes are also used. Stylistic elements that use understatement to emphasize the point of negative connotations to further validate the positive, often incorporating double negative effects. For example, "he does not look bad" could express that someone is beautiful or could convey that he is not particularly ugly or attractive. The degree of emphasis depends on the context. For example, the commonly used phrase "not bad" may indicate that something is either average or excellent. Under the same conditions, litotes can be used to reduce the rigidity of observation: "he is not the tidiest person I know" - used as a means of showing that someone is a disorderly (untidy) person.

We've all heard about the good old metaphors. These are comparisons by which the transfer of meaning is accomplished so as to highlight one common characteristic from one area of life and the world that connects with another area.

The way in which personality types are presented to the masses on the available platform is extremely often reflected in these stylistic figures. Sometimes there is a certain intention behind it, and sometimes it is about presenting the attitude in an authentic way. This attitude is a consequence of knowing about the types of personality that an individual possesses. Knowledge is awareness, understanding of someone or something, such as information, facts, and knowledge is also the experience gained through perception, education, discovery, learning. Education is the formation of personality by adopting different content and values. Perception is a complex and active process of seeking, receiving, processing, organizing and interpreting various stimuli. Learning is the acquisition of relatively permanent and progressive changes in the individual and the behavior of the individual resulting from the individual's previous activity (the so-called "experience"). Learning is a process. With it, we acquire knowledge and modify ourselves.

In concrete examples of personality types, we will see what this is about. Let's start by looking at the INFJ type. The phrase "INFJs forgot living a life of full lungs" is an obvious euphemism. When we say "one of the most enigmatic mystics" instead of "INFJ", we use periphrasis. When the words "mystic", "advisor", "advocate" are used instead of "INFJ", then it is about antonomasia. Dysphemism, or depicting the INFJ type in a more ugly way would be when the ENTP type after a bad experience with the INFJ type says "everything she read between the lines about me was inadequate".

Looking at an ENTP man who had a negative experience with an INFJ woman, I came across a few insights.

He chose the YouTube platform to express himself creatively and interact with people. On the same platform, under the circumstances at the time, the INFJ type was dominant in multiple dimensions. They are extremely numerous there, so they will bring a large number of views to the video that is about them and a provocative context will certainly attract them.

Looking at that person, the impression I most indulged in was that it was important for him to elicit a reaction while enjoying the act of provocation. The success of the video was less important to him (if we consider success as attracting more people to the channel). Many succeeded when they had words of praise for the INFJ type on their channel. What is the cause of this? The question is similar to this one: "which came first the chicken or the egg".

Many of the most popular articles about the INFJ personality type have created a beautified image of what it actually is, to the point that even articles that speak about its flaws are usually accompanied by a rationalization of why those flaws exist and who caused them and induced them...

Were those who started promoting typology in this way (on the Internet) INFJ types who needed uniqueness and their flaws to be turned into virtues? Are they really the "rarest type"? Does being the "rarest type" mean anything good? Is that a euphemism, too?

An ENTP man, aware of this situation, started the adventure of provoking everything that built the perfect image of the INFJ type. Let's look at him critically as well. All the time while attacking every glorified virtue, there is a constant need for justifying himself by saying "I am not saying this to attack you", "I am not saying this to make you cry now", "I am aware of what you can do, it is painful for me to watch what you are doing to yourself by wrong judgments of people, which is why I attack you". The entire presentation was a combination of presenting a concerned tone full of understanding and throwing INFJ quality on the ground. Seeing his inauthentic behavior and obvious intent, I thought there was little chance that the INFJ types who listened to him would not see the same thing I saw.

At the other side, here is an example of how the INFJ flaws are presented in a beautiful way:

"We can be spontaneous, but sometimes we just can't focus our mind on a new idea, sometimes even a sudden change in plans is enough to confuse us. It seems like we're inflexible, but it really takes us a while to be ok with a new plan or idea. " ,

"Know that if an INFJ friend tells you something that you do not want to hear, it is because he is sincerely concerned about you and wants only good for you. Yes, INFJs can be brutally honest, but only rarely malicious. ",

"Often, INFJs are right when they shut someone's door forever. People who emotionally abuse them should beware of them. ",

"It's not easy to be a deeply emotional person in this difficult world. We may have a dark side, but we are capable of loving, being gentle and full of empathy. ",

I can't say that these statements are incorrect. The way things are presented is washed and beautified. Manner and intention are crucial in creating an image. This interesting phenomenon of type glorification, from my perspective, seems to have created a disturbance. What happens is that some people who prioritize their own identity above everything, are going to feel inferior to the ideal and decide to be that "perfect type".

It also happens that those who are aware of this phenomenon and are not sympathizers of it but they actually are real INFJs- are "attacked" by those who do not want the picture to fade away if they express a different attitude.

It also happens that after my typing, a person asks, "Are you sure I'm an INFJ? It seems to me like there are a lot of fake INFJs everywhere and I wouldn't want to be one of them".

There is general collective confusion on the subject. At times it seems to me that some of them are accusing everyone of being a "fake INFJ" who does not fit the idealized image.

Many flaws of the ENFJ type are not mentioned because it is the most similar type to the INFJ type. Does the ENFJ type also create an idealized image in the same way? Or is it just a "sister type" so they "don't touch it"? Probably both. One thing is for sure, much less dust rises for the ENFJ type.

Are any of the 16 types more special than the others? What does it even mean to be a special type? Is that a good thing or a bad thing? Why is this important to many people? Does it matter to many people?

Maybe it all started with Jung ... Maybe it's important that from him it all began. I often think about how ingenious it was of him for what he did. I am immensely grateful to him and admire him. When I was little, I often noticed that some people are almost exactly the same as some I already know and that I don't even have to bother to find out anything specific about them because I can easily compare them. I needed explanations. The various groupings of people seem to me to be very adequate. Adler's clustering is great, but what Jung did was brilliant. Adler divided the types into:

Ruling type - those who push others to gain superiority,

Learning type - those who have obsessions, phobias, are sensitive, who build walls around them,

Avoiding type - those who survive by avoiding life, and

Socially useful type – those who are functional in the world and society;

Looking at these four types, types according to Jung or MBTI types, we could also combine them with Enneagram types (+ Tritype), recall Eysenck and his division into sanguine, choleric, phlegmatic and melancholic and imagine just how many possible combinations of a single personality there is. We are indeed very special and different from each other, but certain frames cannot be avoided. They are very present and active. Just as every beehive with its bees has its own characteristics, arrangement, and natural flows, this world looks like a meadow full of beehives of different sizes and colors, but each is the same inside. Each has its own queen bee, worker bees that have different tasks, and drone-bees who live off the hive. If only government arrangements were as ideal as the bee world... There is no injustice in the bee world. If a mouse enters a hive, they kill it and wrap it so it doesn't stink. In nature, many things are in incredible balance and harmony. There is something wrong with us people. Regardless of the higher level of awareness, of our conscience, it often seems to me that bees are smarter. We are often spoiled, dirty and small. Why are we like that? Countless answers everywhere, but no matter what I read, I think I will ponder it forever…

Each Type description can be drawn through a filter to cleanse it from euphemism and beautification. The INFJ was just a pictorial example that could give us the wider picture. We can observe euphemisms in descriptions of any other type. For example: ESTJ "has a problem putting himself in other people's shoes", ISTJ "has a skeptical view of certain things", ESTP "has a problem to see the domain of his capabilities", ISTP "a problem to see that he has offended someone", INFP "remain to his opinion regardless of the facts to the contrary", ENFP "renounce past", ENFJ "exaggerates things for the effect", INTPs "have difficulty seeing what others need emotionally", ENTPs "deal with small things that don't matter", ENTJs "have difficulty understanding what is good for them", INTJs "may lose the sense of the real world", ISFPs "sometimes have a hard time understanding the situation and reacting to it", ISFJs "sometimes find it difficult to embark on new ways of doing things", ESFPs "sometimes believe in the things they have imagined", ESFJs "care about the opinion of majority".

All these sentences could actually be simplified. Insensitive person, grumpy person, a person full of himself, a person who has no touch with reality, passive aggressor, stubborn person, foolish person, liar, naive person, annoying person, emotionally immature person, dozy person, closed-minded person, paranoid person, a person who lacks his own opinion.

As we can see, these terms and descriptions do not sound gratifying at all.

Samuel Wild

RELATIONSHIPS WITH CAREGIVERS (PARENTS) AND THEIR IMPACT ON TYPE

The being who is born is, in its earliest days, dependent on others in meeting its own needs. Around the age of eight months, the infant becomes able to seek contact with the person who most often cares for him, and this is most often the mother in many cultures. Seeking contact with a caregiver, especially in conditions that the infant perceives as threatening is the core of the attachment. Attachment is an emotional bond that encompasses the various behaviors that the infant seeks in order to maintain closeness with the caregiver. From the perspective of the infant, it wants to gain the experience that there is no danger, to be calmed down, and to be comforted in situations where the infant feels unsafe and scared.

To achieve this effect, the caregiver needs to interpret the infant's signals properly.

Adequate attachment is important for its further development. These early emotional experiences are crucial for mental health, the experience of oneself, and the quality of relationships with people from their environment that this infant will form in the future.

We can talk about attachment disorders when we notice children's reactions that are significantly different from those that are usual, (in contact with a nurturing person and other people in the environment) and these reactions must last for a long period of time in all situations involving such human contact.

Disorganized attachment: These children are characterized by stiffness of all movements, repetition of certain actions, and various forms of disorganization. Their parents were often abusive or mentally ill. Instead of a caregiver, whom protects and gives love to him/her and who s/he can count on, a child has a person that s/he perceives as someone he is afraid of. It is the parent who provides terrifying experiences. Oftentimes, this will be a person who is constantly intimidated, and thus the infant perceives fear and confusion as a common feeling. This creates dissociation in the child, whose self-image becomes divided.

In extreme cases, this caregiver abuses the child: emotionally, sexually, or physically. The child realizes that there is no solution to the fear with which he or she is experiencing and therefore is in a hopeless situation. One side of the brain thinks "I feel fear so I need my caregiver to protect me and calm me down" and the other side of the brain is saying "I feel fear, I have to get rid of what causes my fear". There is a mixed feeling in the child's brain: "the caregiver must be good" and the other is a feeling that he or she should escape from such torment. There is no solution…

These children have problems understanding people later in life. They often misinterpret other people's reactions because their neuro-system has learned from experience that if, for example, a person raises his hand for whatever reason (he waves), he may believe that "she/he raised her/his hand to hit him, to harm him.".

This causes potential reactions:

Total helplessness and numbness

Feeling great fear and escape.

Fighting (violence).

The child wonders if he is helpless, will he run, and if the answer in his head is no, he will fight. The reaction will be impulsive.

Anxious avoidant attachment: occurs when the infant realizes that there is no intention of the caregiver to be close to him. These children experience the image of themselves as beings that are not worthy of their mother's attention and they perceive the world as a place that is not safe. This model of affective attachment can be formed even when the mother is physically present and caring for the child in a particular way, but in a way that is not adequate and related to the child's real needs. For example, the baby can cry because the baby is hungry and the mother is unaware of the real need and covers the baby with the blanket because she thinks the baby is cold.

In order to protect itself from further suffering in life and negative experiences, the child builds a wall between himself and the rest of the world, becomes distanced, distrustful of anyone but himself.

Anxious ambivalent attachment: when the mother selectively responds to the baby's needs, which means, she is not consistent- in some situations she responds and in some she does not. She is either physically absent or simply inconsistent in her reactions.

In such circumstances, the child creates a feeling of distrust because it is not certain that the mother will be there when he needs her. In such circumstances, the infant is forced to constantly fight to gain a mother's attention.

As a consequence, these children are not interested in exploring the environment because they are steadily monitoring their mother in constant fear of abandonment.

Secure attachment: the mother is available, adequately responding to the baby's signals and needs. The child is able to form a positive image of himself and the world. These infants view themselves as beings worthy of love, and the world as a safe place (they believe in themselves, they trust other people, they trust their own abilities, there are safe, confident people).

The attachment that is formed between the caregiver and the child lasts throughout life, affects the child's personality and later his or her relationship with a partner.

It often happens that a person did not have a strictly one pattern of affective attachment, but a combination of several.

I find that certain types are more inclined towards certain models of affective attachment. So, for example, in my case, we can notice a combination of anxious-avoidant attachment, secure attachment, and disorganized attachment.

The ENFJ personality type tends to be a combination of these three. Since I'm Enneagram 4, I'm the closest to the anxious-avoidant model. Anxious avoidant model is often associated with Enneagram 4. The basic fear of this type is to have no identity (to be nobody and nothing). The cause of this fear lies in the neglect of the infant.

An imperceptible infant will want to be a noticeable person. Since he is not noticeable in a regular way, he will look for his own. A similar form of neglection that shaped the ENFJ individual, exists in the formation of the INFP and ISFP individuals.

With reference to my childhood, which has already been briefly discussed, the cause of each of these three models can be seen.

Anxious-avoidant - lack of food and lack of adequate reaction to the problem, lack of interest from the father. Disorganized - growing up in an environment that didn't quite wish me well things in life, a turbulent relationship with my mother (who has narcissistic tendencies, and tendencies towards dependent personality disorder). Secure - this is the percentage I mentioned when I "weighed my childhood". Although the percentage of secure attachment was the highest on tests I took, my subjective feeling is that it may not be adequate because my relationships with people are problematic.

In my teenage years, I felt toxic shame. I did not have normal friendships.

Either I sabotaged them for no reason or I bonded with friends who were not quite close to me empathetically. I sabotaged the emotional connections and predicted the end and my own departure even before the relationship entered a more serious phase. Fear of being close to people followed me like a curse. I watched normal people and felt shame (inferiority).

I will also review the other types.

The ENFP type is most prone to the anxious-ambivalent attachment. They are constantly followed by the fear of losing a loved one and being abandoned.

They are accompanied by the mistrust they feel in relationships and toxic jealousy.

As he or she has been in a constant battle for the mother's attention as an infant, an ENFP as an adult also remains in the constant battle for his or her partner's attention.

It may feel like a person is trying hard (loving too much) and not getting enough in return. The mother's inconsistency causes an inconsistency in the individual himself, ENFP (lack of Si) and a desire for the constant presence of the mother and contempt for her departure (natural attraction to the lack of Se in the partner). They idealize the partner, believing that the positive qualities of the partner will make up for their lackings.

They have a possessive nature. Breakups are hard to bear and they can be prone to self-harm behavior. Not infrequently, ENFP has been designed with a combination of anxious ambivalent attachment and disorganized attachment.

The INFP type is most often derived from anxious-avoidant attachment, but it is also often the combination of multiple models. INFP types are characterized by extreme social inhibition, inadequacy, shame for no reason. They have no confidence, they are closed, and they are afraid of intimacy, even if they often want it badly.

The ISFP type came from a very similar situation. Both types, just like the ENFJ, may be those that attract attention, provoke a reaction, and therein lies an intrinsic fear of people, intimacy (closeness), and sabotaging relationships with people.

INFJ usually has secure attachment as an infant, but it often happens that certain INFJ subtypes have indications of disorganized attachment as a result of emotional abuse. Usually, emotional abuse in their case is an omnipresent mother with narcissistic personality characteristics.

INTP and ISTJ types are a consequence of secure attachment, but examples of anxious-avoidant attachment are also often found. Although these types have generally received adequate care as infants, it happens that their parents were "cold" and "emotionally distant" so that made them cold, indifferent…

In the case of the INTJ and ENTJ types, we will mostly come across secure attachments but the outlines of other models can also be encountered (except anxious ambivalent attachment), particularly in cases where the father figure is far away from or unresponsive towards the infant.

ESFJ and ESTJ generally have secure attachments and often disorganized attachments. The same case is with ESTP and ENTP.

In most cases, ESFP and ISFJ have a secure attachment model and often ESFP has anxious ambivalent attachment.

ISTP has often been formatted by secure attachment or disorganized attachment.

TYPES IN A FRAME

QUADRAS AND RELATIONSHIPS WITH PARENTS

ALPHA QUADRA

Quadra that values Fe/Ti, Ne/Si.
(ESFJ/ESE, ISFJ/SEI, INTP/LII, ENTP/ILE)
I call this quadra the *I want Dad quadra*.

The *I want Dad quadra* is the quadra that wants to be part of a society where it can express its views and ideas and get some answers...

This quadra is focused on information. That is what they feed on. They want information. They will most often watch TV or read all the latest news on the Internet, they will deal with gossip, although INTPs will often scorn them publicly.

So why do I call them the *I want Dad quadra*? Most of these types have an open or secret desire for authority, for someone who will be stronger than them and who will be "their back".

The ISFJ, ESFJ and ENTP are characterized by passivity and a clear need for someone to look after them. They are ready to invoke authority when defending their position. Although normally the lively intellect of xNTP types will question the truth of everything, their opinions will be shaped in a certain way, just like the opinions of xSFJ types, under the strong influence of the opinion of the authority or the opinion of the majority.

You will often come across the naivety of ISFJ and INTP types as well as the frequent unusual idealization of the father figure in ESFJ and ENTP types.

The father is a key figure in the formation of these types even when he does not exist. The need for a father is what is crucial. The common thing for ISFJ and INTP types is the naivety of the child, the common feature of the ESFJ and ENTP types - very often hypochondria. Often these types have highly positioned Enneagram 6. ENTP types can also be characterized by a lack of empathy. ESFJ can too, but it is rare…

Samuel Wild

BETA QUADRA

Quadra that values Fe/Ti, Se/Ni.
(ENFJ/EIE, INFJ/IEI, ESTP/SLE, ISTP/LSI)
I call this quadra *I don't like mom, I don't have dad quadra.*

A lack of motherly love can cause a lack of empathy in a child, but "too much mom" can cause the same effect. Sometimes less is really more.

ISTP and ENFJ usually had this lack of a mother and her adequate love. INFJ and ESTP very often had a "mom on a plate" waiting hand and foot, and so saturation occurred. In the case of the INFJ type, because of their mother "it is hard to breathe" and the ESTP type developed a lack of appreciation, gratitude and even empathy because "mom was served on a plate".

The father is not an important figure here. This quadra likes to get what they want, often with a lack of empathy (even though xNFJs are great empaths, but when they are overwhelmed, used, etc., they happen to block their feelings for others, especially when attacked).

GAMMA QUADRA

Quadra that values Te/Fi, Se/Ni
(ENTJ/LIE, INTJ/ILI, ESFP/SEE, ISFP/ESI)
I call this quadra *I am my own dad and my mom's golden egg.* This is a quadra in which the father is not an important figure. This is usually the quadra of mom's little ones who got all the love, attention and adoration. They are self-oriented and they value the shifts, developments, and progress. They are not interested in belonging to a group per se, but they do not mind the loyalty of others. They actually expect that.

INTJ, ENTJ, and ESFP love to have authority. Each in

its own way. Ambition, pragmatism, or competence often play an important role here. Although the ISFP seemingly lacks interest in personal ambition, they may be most upset when someone gets in the way of their personal development journey. They all know what they want or what they feel.

DELTA QUADRA

Quadra that values Te/Fi, Ne/Si.
(ESTJ/LSE, ISTJ/SLI, ENFP/IEE, INFP/EII)
I call this quadra *I love my mom more than dad*.
Very often, xNFP types will be eager for the mother and have some form of a problematic relationship with the father.

I used the term "eager for the mother" because xNFPs did not have "enough mother" as they needed. On the other hand, xSTJ types have often had "enough mother" but they are very attached to how she feels just like xNFP types.

The inner potential of other people and themselves is very important to them. They like to be free while exploring that potential.

Their relationships, interests and values are important to them. They usually admire the *beta quadra* because of their "courage".

When it comes to type compatibility, attachment theories and this general look at quadras should be kept in mind.

SamuelWild

UNDERSTANDING TYPES, THEORIES AND THEIR CREATORS

Each type is only one descriptive definition of almost all characteristics of an individual. Each type arose as a result of several factors.

Freud spoke about the development of personalities during childhood. According to Freud, the basic motor starter of every personality and every behavior is libido. Libido energy animates the three components that make up personality: id, ego, and superego.

Id represents basic needs and urges. Id is the aspect of personality present at birth.

Ego is the aspect in charge of controlling Id's hints and forcing it to behave in realistic ways. Superego is the ultimate aspect of personality that needs to evolve and contains all the ideals, morals and values imposed on us by our parents and culture. This part of the personality tries to get the Ego to act in accordance with these ideals. Then, Ego must adjust between the true needs of Id, the idealistic standards of the Superego, and reality.

Adler was one of the first psychologists to emphasize the need, distinction, and importance of interpersonal relationships and social factors involved in personality formation. It has been eight decades since the book

"Understanding Human Nature" first appeared in which Adler talked about this. The impact of this book on psychology is huge, ranging from social psychoanalysis to humanistic, existential, and personalistic psychology.

Jung's theory of personality was one of the most significant achievements of modern thought. He, as we know, distinguishes two main attitudes or orientations of personality: extraversion and introversion (orientation to the external and internal world). Both of these opposing views are present in the personality, but usually one of them is more dominant.

What these two psychologists have in common? They have come to general and universal conclusions and insights by observing individual items. These two psychologists were xNFJs, so this approach and look at people strongly embodied the qualities and concepts that make up introverted intuition.

In 1914, Jung separated from Freud and psychoanalysis.

According to Jung, man is a complex being: sexual and religious, instinctive and spiritual, unconscious and conscious, irrational and rational, so forth. Personality is determined by past events as well as future planning. Henceforth, the term used to describe the "unconscious", for Jung, is not only a dump for which abominable urges lay, but also a source of tremendous and deep wisdom. In addition to the "personal unconscious" which includes many inferiorities, in mental life, a particularly important role is inherited and becomes more than personal - "the collective unconscious" that represents all aspects of unconsciousness is experienced by all people of different cultures.

He also mentioned archetypal images – universal symbols that can mediate opposites in the psyche, often found in religious art, mythology and fairy tales across cultures. The unconscious is generally thought of to speak and understand information through said symbols.

His elements are archetypes that are the invisible roots of our overall experience and behavior. Libido is not only sexual, it is also the whole psychic and even life energy itself.

If libido is focused on external reality, it is an attitude and focus of extraversion, and if it is focused on internal reality, then it is the attitude of introversion.

This is the theoretical basis of Jung's typology of personality.

According to Jung, personality develops throughout the whole life, but he has given special attention to the process of spiritual development in the second half of life. He called this (spontaneous self-exploration and self-development) individualization.

Personality is a self-regulatory system that develops through compensation mechanisms, which constantly strive for a more complete balance.

Personality is a semi-open system and therefore there is an exchange of energy with the external environment. Food is taken from it, which is the basis of metabolic processes. The resulting spiritual energy is invested in an external object. The more significant an object or goal is, the greater the amount of mental energy is invested, and this is called mental value.

In Jung's theory, defense mechanisms are represented through the progression and regression of energy. In the process of progression, energy from archetypes go to the "personal unconscious", which then proceeds to charge its contents, before finally delivering them to the "I" (conscious part of the personality). Depending on the dominance of functions and viewpoints, "I" disposes that energy into external objects and moves forward. If there is an obstacle along the way, the "I" cannot rationally cope with the given situation and, for defense, will resort to restoring the energy backwards. This process is called "regression". With the help of regression, the contents are suppressed into the personal unconscious, and energy is stored in a kind of subsystem, which can disrupt the balance if left dormant and suppressed. If the pent up energy is held in a subsystem for too long, the unconscious part of the personality takes control of the "I" and such a person behaves in all sorts of unadaptable mannerisms.

Jung points out that not every regression is negative. The unconscious part contains personal and archetypal experiences, so it can happen that an impoverished person from a difficult situation proceeds to get richer through another successful way of overcoming a crisis.

Moving energy forward also means moving energy from lower, more primitive content to higher and better content, and this process is called "sublimation".

Adler, founder of the School of Individual Psychology, details that two concepts occupy a key place: striving for superiority and a feeling of inferiority.

He believed that there was one motivating force or aspiration that determined a man's behavior. That is the "pursuit of superiority". The cause of this tendency is the already mentioned "feelings of inferiority". All people have a sense of inferiority, more or less. Adler distinguishes two types of inferiority:

Organic inferiority - the fact is that in every human being there are organs that are less or more developed. Also, some people have a disease, physical disability, or a deficiency of sorts. According to Adler, a person responds to organic inferiority by compensating in the following way: an inferior organ strengthens or becomes enlarged, or a person psychologically compensates for an organic problem by developing a particular skill or a certain type of personality.

Another type of inferiority is psychological inferiority, which is more common than organic.

The difference between psychological and organic inferiority is that the psychological does not have to correspond to the objective reality.

A person overwhelmed by a sense of inferiority may

develop an "inferiority complex". Another way of responding to inferiority is the superiority complex. By doing so, the person conceals a sense of inferiority by pretending to be superior. If a person is convinced that he or she is worthless, the only way to make them feel valuable is to make others feel worthless.

Examples of this can reach various levels: offenders, braggarts people in higher positions than others... More drastic examples being: People who feel powerful after committing a murder, bullies, etc...

According to Adler, by developing a sense of community, one man compensates for a sense of inferiority and there by reaches maturity through work, collaboration, and friendship. Failure to overcome said inferiority leads to neurosis.

As I stated in one of the previous chapters, Adler distinguished four basic psychological types: ruling type, learning type, avoiding type, and socially useful type.

According to Adler, the psychological type (lifestyle) is formed by the age of five.

He believes that three childhood situations contribute most to the development of a false life goal:
- Organic inferiority and early diseases
- Spoilage
- Negligence

Unlike Freud, for Adler, personality is not a simple product of the past, but he is of the idea that personality is oriented towards the future.

Adler also believes that man should be seen as a whole, not as a mere sum of its constituent parts. This approach is called holism.

When we analyze the work of these three psychologists through the prism of the MBTI typology, we can clearly see what caused their theories.

Freud, as an ISTJ was a supporter of empiricism, and he insists that any unconscious content was once conscious and that he entered the psyche through experience. Because suppressed content retains its effectiveness, such content affects our conscious lives in a variety of hidden ways. Thus, the source of creativity in all fields is explained by the sublimation of this energy store into acceptable and fertile channels. Neurosis occurs when the normal canal: "repression <--> sublimation" for some reason does not work properly. In this situation, the return to normalcy can be achieved through psychoanalysis. Psychoanalysis is the process of examining the unconscious, led by an analyst, whom stimulates memory and uses fragments of dreams to restore and understand the problematic content that caused the blockage. The assumption is that inconvenient content, once stimulated in consciousness, loses its power to interfere with the normal functioning of the psyche. Most often suppressed are those contents that concentrate on incestuous relationships (son's desire for mother and daughter's for father).

Previously, I mentioned my view of quadras and their relationships with parental figures. I called *delta quadra **I love my mom more than dad***.

Freud shows affection for his mother through his theories, and in the section on the unconscious, he talks about disturbing thoughts, memories and urges, including incest.

He also cites hatred for brothers, sisters, parents, and spouses...

The essence of his theory lies in Introverted sensing (Si), because he says that every subconscious content has become conscious and has entered the psyche through the experience, he also evidently shows his relations with Extroverted intuition (Ne) and Introverted sensing (Si)-talking about "the impact of suppressed content on conscious life seeps through various hidden ways".

He designed psychoanalysis to practically solve the problem: to enter the unconscious, see what was happening, to bring it out to consciously and to solve the problem.

Unlike him, his disciple, Jung, separated himself from Freud's teaching. He refused to accept Freud's definition of the unconscious as a dumping ground of abominable urges, because Jung also saw it as a source of wisdom. I think that one can clearly see their differing views on intuition. Jung, as an INFJ, believes that intuition guides him, and he experiences intuition as a source of wisdom. When he talks about "moving energy forward", he says it's a shift from lower, more primitive content to higher and better content. His (Ni) and (Se) relationship is evident enough.

Freud said that maturity and the avoidance of individual nervousness are achieved through the practice of religion. In his understanding, religion is the projection of the father with his prohibitions and orders into cosmic dimensions. Holding onto an illusion and participating in mass neurosis, they can often avoid individual neurosis.

This claim leads me to two thoughts. The first is the apparent skepticism of an ISTJ personality, who perceives religiosity as a "capture for some illusion". A second thought, however, leads me to my view of *alpha quadra*, which alleviates anxiety with a figure of authority...

Jung, an INFJ, found religion more complex. The concept of God is a necessary psychological function for Jung. In his terminology, it is irrational in nature and it is unrelated to the question of proving God. It is not a pathological phenomenon but a basic condition of mental health.

Adler, an ENFJ, also couldn't agree with Freud that personality is a simple product of the past, but a personality is oriented towards the future. Here, we can see a distant relationship with (Si) and an outlook directed in favor of what lies ahead (Ni).

Introverted intuition also confirms his holistic approach to observing personality - that personality should be seen as a whole, not as a simple sum of its constituent parts.

His theory of inferiority is also based on understanding people from a very personal perspective. I have already talked about my own inferiority and difficulties in growing up. I'm am ENFJ. He was also an ENFJ.

Adler's attitude is that man compensates for inferiority by developing a sense of community, and upon reaching maturity through work, collaboration and friendship, as I stated earlier. This approach demonstrates the obviousness of the Extraverted feeling (Fe) function.

With the strong influence of Adler's view, that being that the psychological type is formed by the **age of five**, with key concepts:

- Organic inferiority and early diseases
- Spoilage
- Negligence

as well as John Bowlby's theory (attachment theory), I came to some understanding of type compatibility, but also pathology in typology (personality disorders conditioned by a social factors).

COMPATIBILITY OF TYPES IN EMOTIONAL RELATIONSHIPS AND PATHOLOGY IN TYPOLOGY

There is no ideal compatibility of types because there are no ideal types as such, but we should not avoid the fact that some types are better suited to other types…

I often watch talk shows, especially those with many guests. I like to observe and analyze their behaviors and look for hidden meanings, their intentions and so on...

It is very interesting to observe similarities in reactions and behaviors of the same types, but it is the most interesting to me when I can observe compatible types who complement each other, admire each other, and sometimes even flirt, consciously or unconsciously.

For some reason, I enjoy that very much.

Things are very connected and yet simple, though they are seemingly complicated. I notice several types of attraction among types.

One is the attraction of the tertiary function. We like to see our tertiary function when it is dominant in someone. Our dominant functions are what we were released to develop from an early age, and we have developed this function by force of circumstances (depending on our destiny, circumstances, and our types). They lead us, we are subordinate to them and we are condemned to them.

The third function, the tertiary function, is what we are not the best at, but we are very proud to use it, especially when we use it successfully. We are often unable to see how good or bad we are when it comes to using the third function.

When we look at someone who uses our third function as dominant, we actually see what we could be. As a kid who plays. It is akin to a kid that pretends to be a doctor and then sees a real doctor and thinks, "Well, this is what I want to be. I admire this."

The ESFP/ENFP admires the ENTJ/ESTJ when speaking directly, realistically, and without reservation.

The ISFP/ISTP admires the INTJ/INFJ because of the depths they touch naturally, without much effort.

The INTJ/ISTJ admires the INFP/ISFP for their authenticity and loyalty to their feelings.

The INFJ/ISFJ admires the INTP/ISTP for logically observing things.

The ENFJ/ENTJ admires the ESFP/ESTP for their sense of the present moment.

The ESTP/ENTP admires the ENFJ/ESFJ for their relentless feelings for others.

The INFP/INTP admires the ISFJ/ISTJ for their consistency, ability to "master" what they do.

The ESFJ/ESTJ admires the ENTP/ENFP because of their naturalness as they adapt to change.

So, for example, an ENFJ will be charmed by an ESFP, as the ENFJ will admire Se in the ESFP, but the ESFP will see flaws in the ENFJ's Se.

The ENFJ will be amazed with Se in the ESTP with a slightly lower intensity.

Why the lower intensity? Because ESTP has Fe in third place, so ENFJ, in addition to admiring Se, still feels a hold on Fe as third and weaker function.

The same logic can be applied to any given example.

INTP person will be sympathetic in an INFJ's eyes because of their sharp Ti, and the ISTP, although sympathetic, because their Ni is in third place, they will still not sympathize as well as the INTP. Et cetera...

However, much more attraction exists between types whose functions are as they are (Fe/Ni, Se/Ti) and the second type whose functions are "inverted" compared to the first type (Fi/Ne, Si/Te). It is a well-known rule of attraction and compatibility, which is generally accepted but often comes under criticism (because of people's bad experiences).

What lies behind this form of compatibility? Let's remember QUADRAS to begin with.

Alpha quadra (ESFJ, ISFJ, INTP, ENTP) which I called **I want Dad quadra** uses Fe/Ti, Ne/Si and naturally attracts with *gamma quadra* (ENTJ, INTJ, ISFP, ESFP) which I called **I am my own dad and my mom's golden egg** (Te/Fi, Se/Ni).

The *beta quadra* (ENFJ, INFJ, ESTP, ISTP), I called **I don't like mom, I don't have dad quadra,** uses Fe/Ti, Ni/Se, and is naturally attracted to the *delta quadra* (ESTJ, ISTJ, INFP, ENFP) I called **I love my mom more than dad** (Te/Fi, Ne/Si).

<u>NF types:</u>

Let us look at ENFJs and INFJs and their compatibility with INFPs and ENFPs.

In the case of ENFJ and INFP types, we find compatibility, and the causes of which I will explain.

I believe that in order for an NF type to develop from infancy, some distress or trauma must occur. Someone is not an idealist by accident. It is not by accident that people are strongly turned to people and opportunities they carry with them. In order for Feeling and Intuition functions to guide you, you had to go through something that trained you for it. It is no coincidence that xNFJ types are able to "read minds", "perceive what's behind", "connect dots and see the essence of an image". It is a training that started in the early stages of growing up, and often in the earliest stages...

<u>Example ENFJ-INFP</u>:

Adler spoke of inferiorities. Inferiority plays a crucial role in the case of these two types. Sometimes they are organic or are early diseases, sometimes they are psychological (and may have nothing to do with objective reality), sometimes it involves neglecting individuals, and sometimes it is a combination of some or all of these.

The relationship with the mother of the individual is very complex and crucial (determining) when it comes to the ENFJ individual. In addition to some of these forms of inferiority, the ENFJ is generally the victim of some form of emotional abuse by the mother figure. In most cases, they are narcissistic mothers. In such circumstances, the ENFJ individual develops increased sensitivity for the needs of others, inability to express what s/he thinks (and at the same time develops various defense mechanisms), shyness and a desire to prove oneself, and a lack of a sense of self. The ENFJ type needs an understanding of which the person has never had, a lack of criticism, and total acceptance of the person's flaws, as well as a focus on his or her own heart.

The INFP individual has typically went through a similar situation, except that the relationship with the mother in the case of INFP is much less problematic.

Both types, due to their own sense of inferiority, tend to have avoidant personality disorder tendencies and also histrionic personality disorder tendencies. They want connection and attention but they are afraid of it.

ENFJs very often become victims of narcissistic emotional abuse.

Freud's phrase "scar of a narcissist" is the reaction of a narcissist to an injury that he experienced when someone disturbed his confidence and self-worth (self-image).

Both of these types are extremely sensitive to criticism. The ENFJ often does not want to hear criticism in the face. Thus, an INFP that does not speak directly (inferior Te) but does so passively makes it easier to bear for the ENFJ. For fear that harmony will be disturbed, something that an ENFJ individual needs with as much desperation as air itself, does not allow his/herself use criticism in relation to others, but rather makes his or her presence flattering and pleasing to others. In this way, the ENFJ unconsciously protects oneself from disharmony, tension, and conflict, because by his own imposition of harmony he controls the situation. The INFP finds this feature extremely attractive. The INFP also admires the fierce independence and strong willed determination that the ENFJ has, and the ENFJ admires the gentle authenticity and honesty of the INFP individual. When they aren't judging each other, they feel safe because that's what they needed and craved growing up. It is this understanding that may provide them with peace and closeness. The ENFJ's autonomy and narcissistic tendencies will make her/him want to "exploit" the depth of emotions of an INFP person, who usually has a tendency for dependent personality disorder. The INFP is prone to idealization, which inspires the ENFJ to try even harder. An INFP person, due to a negativistic view on life will find the natural optimism of the ENFJ person attractive. The appeal of these two types can be seen both in the way they talk and how they "recognize" each other. A great deal of understanding, avoiding conflicts, and their strong values is what is crucial in bringing them together. Both types tend to "escape from the realistic observation of things" and instead prefer to use different styles of imagination.

Although such combinations are usually almost ideal (although the ideal does not truly exist), they are often fatal and unsustainable, especially with NF types. Problems that can be addressed are: lack of authenticity of the ENFJ (which causes stress to the INFP person) and passive aggression of the INFP (which causes tension and therefore stress to the ENFJ).

What is irresistible to these types is the conversation that can effortlessly flow with such perfection and naturalness. It will allow the two to indulge in a cozy, familiar atmosphere, but can still give challenges in terms of thinking (intuitive concepts). The ENFJ needs a good listener, and no one is a better listener than the INFP person. The INFP knows best why many ENFJs are called "the giver", and the ENFJ knows well why INFPs are called "the healer".

Relationships can be exciting and deep, but also fatal, and the sustainability of a relationship depends on the health level of both types.

ENFJ tendencies: narcissism, histrionic pd, avoidant pd.

INFP tendencies: avoidant pd, histrionic pd, negativistic PD, dependent personality disorder.

In a worst case scenario, which may not even be rare, a narcissistic ENFJ often ends up with a dependent INFP.

When they are not attracted? When one of these two types is completely smitten by unhealthy tendencies and the other type is healthy.

Also, probably: When the ENFJ is an Enneagram 2 and the INFP is an Enneagram 4.

When ENFJ is Enneagram 3 and INFP is Enneagram 9.

We should, of course, take into account that people are quite complex and that this is only a general framework to base compatibility on. Each MBTI type has a subtype, and each subtype varies in theme…

<u>Example ENFP-INFJ</u>:

The attachment model of ENFP persons, which is insecure/ambivalent attachment, at an early age, leaves the consequences that arise and are reflected in the specificity of needs in emotional relationships. Selective response to the needs of the infant and inconsistency in responding to its needs will create an inconstant individual. These circumstances create a sense of distrust as well as an expressed fight for attention later in life and in relationships with others. The repercussions also include an unstable self-image, a strong fear of abandonment, and even a voided sense of emptiness and despair.

To have peace of mind, an ENFP individual sees the ideal partner in someone who will not provoke these painful points of personality. That is someone who will not be bothered by his need for attention, his inconsistency, distrust, fear of abandonment, and frequent changes of the self-image.

Why is this an INFJ? An INFJ is a person who finds mistrust (jealousy) interesting and appealing and does not mind being entertained; moreover, it is much more desirable than to entertain, so the spotlight certainly belongs to the ENFP person. Inconsistency and frequent changes for the INFJ mean a more dynamic life than she/he is used to having.

In cases of "ideal compatibility", flaws (inferior functions) are also attracted.

Inferior Se means safety for an ENFP because the ENFP "evokes early memories of the caregiver's departure" in a relationship. Inferior Se also indicates that the INFJ lacks interest in attracting attention. INFJ had a consistent nurturing figure, sometimes even "too consistent". INFJs' caregiver (most often a mother) is someone who is often too involved in the life of the INFJ. Just like the ENFJ, the INFJ is often the product of a narcissistic mother. Although there are significant differences between the two types, it is certain that both types were forced to develop Ni and Fe in order to "survive". The INFJ, therefore, "must know" how someone feels and why it is so. They don't need a concrete or direct answer to what comes to them (Te - blind spot).

Due to their suppressed Se and Te (blind spot), the INFJ individual also has the inglorious characteristics of indecisiveness and passivity, yet also a sense of emptiness and often depression. INFJs are, in many cases, an extension of their mothers without which they cannot decide for themselves with certainty. Because their mothers were too heavily involved with the INFJ's life segments, they do not like to "be left alone in the world". Because of the jealousy of the ENFP due to its own insecurity, it may give the INFJ the feeling that the ENFP is extremely concerned about them. ENFPs are decisive and this is also appealing to INFJs. It is attractive to the INFJ that the ENFP is inclined to idealize the partner. Si (inferior) is attractive to an INFJ because it brings dynamics to her/his life. Both types struggle with feelings of emptiness, which gives them closeness and understanding when it comes to looking at the world.

Just like with ENFJ and INFP, in these two types, what is visible in explosive chemistry is rapid recognition, overlapping energies, conversations that flow naturally and that are also challenging in terms of intuitive concepts and ideals.

The ENFP secretly wants to be "read" and "treated according to that feeling" and also desires honest advice, and the INFJ wants to feel special, understood and safe... The INFJ also wants to be motivated and uplifted.

Problems can also occur with these two NF types because of the intensity of attraction with fatal outcomes. They occur when, as I have already stated, one of these two types has completely overcome his or her unhealthy tendencies.

Both types can be narcissistic and depressed. ENFPs may also be hypomanic (just like other ExxPs). The INFJ type can be highly dependent in an emotional relationship (passivity). Toxic jealousy can stifle love. The impulsiveness of the ENFP can impair the harmony that the INFJ needs. An unstable ENFP (one with an unstable self-image) can be manipulated by a calculated, narcissistic INFJ...

So why are other NF type combinations not as ideal?

INFP and INFJ -> both passive, the INFP does not

want as much attachment and closeness, and the INFJ finds avoidance unattractive. INFP may perceive a lack of spontaneity (Se) as inauthenticity or boredom, INFJ may perceive Si as boredom. Both types have a hard time making decisions and INFPs have a hard time to endure the criticism of tertiary Ti.

ENFP and ENFJ -> communication problem (neither is interested in listening). The ENFP may perceive Se in the ENFJ as a "betrayal". An ENFJ has a hard time tolerating someone making and playing games through jealous scenes- not trusting an ENFJ could be stressful for him or her.

An ENFJ is not interested in being overly close to someone, and to the ENFP, inferior Ti of the ENFJ is perceived as insincerity.

"ENFP and INFP" and "INFJ and ENFJ" matches are also not ideal combinations for many reasons, but firstly it should be noted that it is because they belong to the same QUADRAS and therefore the dynamic is not the best, nor the most interesting.

<u>Example of ENTJ and INTP</u>:

The ENTJ is a type from quadra whom I called *I am my own dad and my mom's golden egg* and the INTP is from quadra which I called "I want dad". Maybe the QUADRAs names themselves say a lot...

Both types are characterized by a sort of sheltering emotions under the carpet and addressing ratio. Both types find stressful situations in ones that are filled with emotion. Both types find it difficult to make connections with incompetent people.

The ENTJ doesn't feel that he/she cannot in some way impose the energy of a leader.

Both types tend to find "small talk" difficult and stressful.

The INTP is a person who values truth, information, and rational reasoning, and therefore an ENTJ that is prone to critically address a situation that will be cruel to many other types, is going the be interesting, correct, and appealing to an INTP. The INTP will admire the organizational skills and adaptability in the outside world that the ENTJ person so clearly possesses, and the ENTJ will find an INTP's critical thinking and creative logic to be appealing, if not somewhat enticing.

Problems may arise if the ENTJ wants to control the INTP, or if the INTP loses "touch with reality".

Example ENTP and INTJ:

Just like the previous two types, these two types have a hard time dealing with people who they find incompetent.

The ENTP is a type that is often characterized by dependence and passivity, as well as ungratefulness.

The INTJ does not have a problem with this because he/she makes decisions on his/her own accord as a real *I am my own dad*. The INTJ will often have narcissistic tendencies, but also paranoid tendencies, so it is very important that a partner is loyal (which *alpha quadra* can certainly boast about).

As long as an ENTP is loyal to an INTJ, they will have no problem with ungratefulness or a lack of empathy (ENTP has antisocial tendencies).

Their conversations are extremely dynamic, logically-creative and deep. The INTJ has high standards for many things in life and does so as well in terms of a partner. One of the things they crave is the dynamic that which an ENTP with a lot of energy and lively intellect certainly has.

Problems, of course, can and do arise if one of these two types is unhealthy (or both) and it may happen that an unhealthy INTJ completely convinces the ENTP that s/he is insufficiently capable and confident, or if unhealthy ENTP manipulates an INTJ to gain material benefit or other goods.

Example ESFJ and ISFP:

Both types hardly tolerate criticism (conflicts) and lack of appreciation.

The ESFJ feels his/herself as useful when s/he can

serve others unreservedly, and especially likes when others are grateful for that. The thing that will appeal to the ESFJ is for someone to show them that they need them. The ISFP is a very passive type and that is appealing to the ESFJ. The ISFP is also the type that is extremely modest and that trait is very appreciated by the ESFJ.

ESFJs like to talk about their suffering and it is important for them that someone truly understands them and feels what they are saying deeply.

The ISFP will admire the organizational skills and extraverted nature of the ESFJ, and the ESFJ will admire the ISFP's sense of self and strong convictions.

Problems can happen if an ESFJ imposes too much rigidity and structure on the ISFP or does not respect him or her sufficiently, and problems can also arise if the ESFJ feels he or she is losing trust in someone or something they are involved with (for example if the ISFP is cheating on the ESFJ).

Both types may have a problem with the decision-making process, so it may happen that "a third person can get involved" in their relationship.

<u>Example ISFJ and ESFP</u>:

The ISFJ is also one of such passive types so s/he does not prefer to be the leading and decisive figure in a relationship. Despite ISFJs, some other types also have a tendency to depend on others: INFP, ISFP, INFJ, ENTP, and ESFJ.

The ISFJ is looking for support and strength in a partner. S/he needs positive feedback and a sense of security. The ISFJ is attracted to the untamed nature of Se possessed by ESFPs. Spontaneity, cheerfulness, determination, commitment, proficiency, skillfulness; these are all noble qualities to such an individual…

The ESFP expects loyalty. He often has paranoid tendencies when it comes to many aspects of life. Relationships are one of them. The composure and consistency of the ISFJ person instills in him certainty (Si over Ne).

The ISFJ loves to belong to someone/something and likes to do things in a clearly defined way (lack of Te). Eagerly, the ESFP can tolerate this lack of Te because s/he does not like to be imposed rules or to be criticized ... The ISFJ is often a source of wisdom and practicality for the reckless ESFP.

Problems arise if the ESFP has double standards, whereby upon expecting complete commitment and loyalty from the ISFJ and does not adhere to such vows itself.

Issues also surface if an ESFP, by its own risky behavior, violates the security of the ISFJ or if an ISFJ insists on making plans...

<u>Example ESTJ and ISTP</u>:

Both types do not tolerate irrational behavior. Neither do they tolerate emotional situations (environment = filled with emotions). Both types do not enjoy being too bothered by intuitive or theoretical concepts.

Avoiding this in the same intensity, both types find the perfect balance in communication together. What can seem cruel or harsh to many types will make sense to these types. The direct and precise planning and organizational skills of the ESTJ are attractive to the ISTP, and the bold determination and deadly sharpness of the ISTP are attractive to the ESTJ.

The problem arises when the ESTJ begins to control the ISTP, who, otherwise, has a great authority resistance. Not to mention, when the ESTJ imposes a rigid structure or tries to forbid him/her something, or when the ISTP is too passive-aggressive and views any request as an opportunity for procrastination; these all lead to issues and dilemmas.

<u>Example ESTP and ISTJ</u>:

The main features of an ISTJ person are the stoic worldview, good submission of criticism, consistency, honesty, and diligence.

If ISTJs are typical "good students" in this life, then what attracts them is the complete opposite. ESTPs do not stand by anyone's rules and they do things the way they want without a second thought.

The ISTJ finds this trait attractive, for he or she has the very problem of being spontaneous, carefree, and relaxed, and thus, enjoys watching someone being those things that truly give off a vibe of being alive.

Most ESTPs have an extremely high opinion of themselves, often to arrogant proportions (narcissistic and antisocial tendencies), to which ISTJ's stoic and skeptical view of the world is completely indifferent towards.

An ESTP that has antisocial tendencies tends to "isolate" a partner from the world and family in some way, to which the rather indifferent ISTJ (schizoid tendencies) is prepared. The ISTJ as a workaholic has the need to accomplish its purpose in concrete gestures so that his/her material utilization or exploitation for the interests of the ESTP does not fall too difficult (but only if the ISTJ sees some subjective sense (Fi) in its proceedings).

The ESTP appreciates the ISTJ's unstressed and independent thinking and often views Si as the wisdom that can prevent him/her from making impulsive decisions.

The problem arises when the ISTJ "kills the vibe" of a delirious ESTP with its seriousness and suspicion, as well as when the ESTP makes the ISTJ feel like he is "living in chaos" (frequent changes, demanding that the ISTJ do what he does not want).

We see that what we might find as intolerable, to others, that is extremely attractive and just what they need. One man's trash is another man's treasure. Beauty is solely in the eye of the beholder, so before we condemn it, let us remember this thought. The INFJ may despise "closed-minded people", but that is exactly what the ESTP will be sympathetic to. The ISTJ will perceive the lack of spontaneity in the INFJ as unattractive, but the ENFP will, therefore, understand it in a very attractive way.

An ENFJ will seem irrational to an ESTJ, but an INFP will understand it all the same... It goes on. You can think about any example and draw conclusions on your own.

TYPING PEOPLE IN CASES WHERE I DON'T OBSERVE THEIR BODY LANGUAGE AND FACIAL EXPRESSION

<u>Example 1:</u>
Hello there
Sara, I'd like your opinion…
Could you type me?
Have you ever done the test before?
I've done multiple ones. I remember scoring ESTJ last time I took 16 personalities.
Do you think you could be any other type?
Well maybe ENTJ, maybe INTJ (I've had suggested that to me few times) or some other high Te type. I am pretty sure I have a pretty high Te.
What is more annoying to you:
-having to be a follower instead of a leader
-lack of control?
Lack of control. I find myself trying to get control over the group even if I try to lay low or find others who try to take the control annoying.

But I do kind of see both to be connected. Having to be a follower instead of a leader is giving up control to some degree, I think.

Is dealing with abstract or theoretical concepts stressful for you?

It can be but it depends. If the situation demands more concrete concepts then it might stress me but otherwise I can find them interesting.

What's your biggest fear?

I think it is to be perceived as weak and people taking advantage of that

What motivates you the most?

Being strong and independent.

What do you dislike in other people?

People who don't seem to understand the consequences of their actions. People who people please too much or care too much of others liking them.

Describe your relationship with your mother (briefly).

We can joke around and have fun together and I have a pretty good relationship right now. I go to her if I have problems but I rarely do because I dislike looking for help.

Describe your relationship with your father (briefly).

I've had fights with him when I was younger so I think our relationship is quite shaky because of that. We're not very close but we can still have fun together. I hardly ever discuss personal problems with him because he isn't the best with emotional support.

How your ideal partner should look like?

They should be able to handle conflict and confrontation, and shouldn't be scared to face my anger. I do want them to be trustworthy and honest with me.

Have you ever felt like you don't know what's good for you?

Hmm yeah. At least when I'm stressed I can get kind of lost with what is good for me.

Are you ambitious?

Yeah. Many people including myself describe me as ambitious. I have a long-term goal which I have and am currently working towards.

How do you feel when people around you lack ideas for the future?

I don't really understand those people. I get stressed about it, because I'd feel lost in their case.

What's your least favorite type? Tell me why.

Based on the types I've met it's probably ESFP. They were wild and didn't think much about the consequences and then they just seemed to be stuck in self-pity once the consequences didn't fit their expectations. The ones I've met gave also been very egocentric, loud and easily offended.

How do you feel when people are lazy?

Annoyed. Irritated.

You seem like an ENTJ

Ah, okay thanks.

You're welcome anytime.

Example 2:

Hey, I found your videos on YouTube a few years ago, I was really interested in the way you dissected the ENTP cause that was my type and I was just in a frenzy to gather information about it. Last time I did it I was ENTP 7w8 always looking forward to knowing myself better and to find a way to connect with my inner thoughts but all of sudden I began to feel more and more isolated, more and more in my head spinning around I was losing my outgoing characteristics and my natural curiosity went into other things so I lost track of a bunch of pieces that defined who I was.

I tested myself again yesterday and I got INFP, do you think that someone can change that much? I mean it's kind of obvious you can but the way that I grew apart from a more innocent me it kind of shock me. I'm 19.

So yeah, the world is a vampire?

Hi ☺ Do you want me to type you?
Yes, that would be awesome.
What's your biggest fear?
My biggest fear is not being able to be in control of the situation. But not in the way I'm a control freak but in the sense of being passed over or humiliated.
What's your biggest motivation?
Freedom.
To be independent.
Do you tend to avoid people?
Yes.
What makes you do that?
Most of the times I feel like they may have nothing interesting to say.
I don't do much of small talk.
Do you often feel bored?
Most of the time.
What do you admire in other people?
I admire when someone has a high value of himself.
What would you change about yourself?
Being less judgmental, in the sense of analyzing every aspect of a person and think that my conclusion is what they really are.
How would you describe your energy?
Seductive, until I get to know the person as a whole until I get bored and just dip.
Thank you for honest answers. You seem like an ENTP. I think you maybe tend to dislike authorities (who would like to control you) just like INFPs do. Maybe that's why you felt confused?
Maybe that's why maybe because I kind of like quiet people.
I like people that can collect themselves in a cool way and when it comes to men they are always quiet, masculine dudes.
When it comes to women, I like silent women too.

Women who can show me new things and keep it mysterious in a way.

Example 3:

Hi Sara! I'm a fan of your YouTube channel and really fascinated by your videos and MBTI. I was wondering if you would type me ☺ I haven't really been able to figure it out myself, and I heard most tests are unreliable.

Hi ☺ Thank you for watching my channel. I could type you, why not. Tell me when you're ready!

I'm ready now, thanks!

Cool. Have you ever done the test before?

Yeah, but I've gotten different results.

Have you ever got an INTJ as your result maybe?

Yes. But also INFP.

Ok. I will ask you some questions if you don't mind.

Sure.

How do you feel when you have to work with people who may seem ignorant or lazy?

I get frustrated. But I usually keep my frustration to myself.

How do you feel in unfamiliar environments?

I feel more at home and more myself in unfamiliar environments, especially in foreign countries.

Why?

I think that people from foreign countries are more excepting of me particularly in Europe (I'm from the U.S.) and I feel more stimulated by new environments. I meant "accepting".

What would make you feel opposite?

I feel stressed when I think I'm trapped in a certain place or situation. Like a job where I have to do the same thing every day, and especially when I was in high school since I didn't have a choice.

Are you Enneagram 4 maybe?

Yes.

I understand that. I am 4 too.
Do you dislike too much noise or sensory input?
Awesome! I think I'm a friend with a lot of 4's. Yes, once I lived near a construction site and it drove me crazy, but it didn't seem to bother my roommates.
What is your favorite cognitive function?
It is hard to say but I get the sense my favorite celebrities have high Ne. I loved Robin Williams and Johnny Depp as a child.
What is your least favorite cognitive function?
I think Ti. As I understand it, I hate when people criticize me for not being accurate or logically consistent.
Do you have struggled with making decisions by yourself?
Yes, I am always asking people for advice even for simple things on how to respond to texts from a girl I like.
Do you ever feel like you are depending on someone?
Yes, I feel I'm dependent on many people. One because I'm not financially secure enough at the moment to live independently, and also I have a few friends I depend to feel certain that what I want to do is okay.
Tell me about that relationship with your friends... In which way you depend on them?
I would say I tend to feel weak because I can get easily depressed when I things don't happen the way I want, and sometimes I lack confidence in myself because I feel like I'm not a good person. But my friends like me a lot and some often tell me I don't know how good I am. So maybe depend on them for validation.
Are you suspicious?
Yes, I have a tendency to be suspicious of people's motives including my own. Like this girl, I dated for a short while broke up with me and I became suspicious of her reasons and I started over-analyzing everything she said.

Did you ever have delusion-like ideas?

Yeah, I think I have delusions of grandeur like dreaming of writing the perfect novel and becoming discouraged when my prose doesn't sound like Tolstoy ☺

I think you are an INTJ. Your Fi seems developed, that's why you probably feel like an INFP sometimes.

<u>Example 4</u>:

Hi Sara. Could you please type me? I found you on YouTube.

Hi ☺

I could type you. Tell me when you're ready!

Ready ☺

The first time I've done test was when I was 25, I was in college back then studying psychology. The result was ISTJ. The second time I did the test when I was 30 and the result to this day was ISFJ.

What type do you think you could be?

I think I am a feeler. But I also had a consultation with a professional and he said that I am an extrovert. He said I am an ENFJ.

Have you ever done the Enneagram test? What type are you?

Yes. 1w9

Ok. How do you feel when you have to work/talk with close minded people?

I feel okay. I respect their opinion. They won't be my best friends though.

Why?

Because the world is constantly changing and people too. I'm studying behavioral analysis now and even when you do an experiment on people there is a threat to social validity called maturation which means that the same test on the same person won't give you the same results because as a person grows his beliefs are changing. If a person is not changing he is not getting better. I think those people are not that smart.

Do you prefer to entertain others or to be entertained?

To be entertained ☺ People often say that I have a poker face because I control my emotions.

But with my close friends I can be an entertainer sometimes.

How do you feel in emotionally charged situations?

Totally fine. I've got everything under control. There has been a situation when I was in situations like that and I never lose my head. I often think if I was on the twin towers on 9/11 I wouldn't just stand there and pray. I would do something.

How does it feel to deal with abstract or theoretical concepts?

I always have a problem with this one. What does it mean abstract concept? Could you give an example?

Something that you can't touch – like "love" and "freedom"?

General ideas or understanding of something...

Can I talk about other civilizations? Yes, I can. Can I talk about astronomy – yes. Can I talk about what I would do if something unrealistic happened – yes.

Yes, in this case, I love abstract concepts!

How do you react to frequent changes?

I don't like the changes. I hate it.

It's not that I follow my plan. Although I do plan my day. Sometimes I postpone things. But I will be reluctant to do something if I wasn't ready for it. I need some time to get ready. For example, if it's a date or I need to go to work unexpectedly I would whine and sometimes I'll go but mostly I won't.

Do you find it hard to be spontaneous?

Yes. It's very hard. But my friend is an INTP and he's very spontaneous and I just love that!!! I'm trying to be spontaneous too because it's fun. I am really trying to do something I haven't planned.

Is it hard to do things if you don't see the point in doing them?
Oh yes! You ask really good questions!
Yes, it's really hard. It's stupid for me.
Thanks ☺ Are you afraid to be alone?
Nope.
Do you actually enjoy being alone?
But once I was staying at home with my son for a whole week and I got depressed because I wanted to go outside and socialize. And another time during summer I spent a whole month alone at home and it was really depressing. I even talked with myself and recorded myself on a video camera because I just felt as if I am mute.

I love socializing but I get tired of it fast. I hate phone talks. I rather meet a person in the real world. But I can't socialize everyday – it just drains me. I enjoy spending time at home, I play video games, watch movies, and I write a blog. But I can't be alone for more than two days. I often get 60/40 introversion/extroversion.

I understand that... I am ambivert myself. Do you often rely on other people for comfort, reassurance, advice, support?
Yes, I do this a lot. I need validation, I need words of comfort.

My INTP is not using words and emotions much and I often call all of my friends. That's just crazy. I call all of them and ask their opinion – what should I do? – what did he mean?

I am often afraid to make a mistake.
Have you ever felt like you lack interest in social relationships?
I used to when I just started socializing at the age of 28. But now I'm totally fine.
Are you good at reading people's intentions?
Usually yes. But not with INTP. I can read intentions and mood very well. I can inspire people, motivate them.

I worked as a teacher in elementary school and children loved me and their parents loved me too.

I often tell people what they want to hear and they like that.

How do I know what they want I can't explain.

I just listen to then talk and boom I know.

Are you often indifferent to criticism?

If it's constructive – yes, I like that. But if I feel it's not true I get upset. Because it means a person is not appreciating what I do.

Lots of people need words of appreciation these days.

Even my INTP.

Do you think you are skeptical?

Sometimes. It's because of my knowledge of psychology. Like for instance, I have huge arguments with an INTJ.

He says that it's okay to clone people and have robots in the future. He also said that he would love to live forever. And I said that he won't like that because his close people will die and he will see death. And he was like, no I will get used to it. I know that he will – but at the point when he will get used to deaths he is going to be so mentally ill – it's just not worth it. When someone talks about psychology or relationship in an abstract way or like this and this will happen – I often get skeptical because that's not the way it works. Yes, I like being skeptical because we just can't know everything for sure until it really happens. But if someone gives me facts and research that has been done I'll listen.

How do you look at people who live in the moment?

They kind of inspire me… Sometimes. I would like to be like that. My two friends are like that and they are so optimistic and happy. My friend left her daughter and bought a one-way ticket to the guy she liked and lived with him in Germany for several years until they got married and then she took her daughter to live with them. When she told me she bought a one-way ticket and spend all the money I was like "wow!!! No, I would never spend all the money and leave my child". But on the other hand, children are so selfish these days they don't appreciate all the sacrifices we made. And money. I save them and then eventually spend them on something that I don't want. And my life is so planned. This is why I like to hang out with spontaneous people. They make me feel happy, they open up the world to me and I become like a child – so excited as if I'm seeing the world for the first time.

Are you nostalgic?

Yes.

Do you have a good memory? You can remember details...?

I don't know certain moments I think about them because I had strong feelings. Details about how I felt... smell and the sound.

But not like details what someone did.

I won't remember the movie or a book for instance.

More of an experience.

I think that you are an ISTJ.

It was really nice to talk to you and to type you. I enjoyed it ☺

Really? Wow! So the first time the test was right. Thanks.

I had a really great time talking to you, too.

Example 5:

Hi Sara, is it a good time for you to do the typing now? Or anytime today? I was busy on the weekend and didn't want to bother you at weird times. Thanks!

I can do it now. I am not busy. Have you ever done the test before?

Many thanks! Yes. I am quite sure I am an INFP, but I think I don't have enough knowledge about myself or how the functions on me, and I get confused, so I'd like an outsider perspective.

Sorry to bother you, since I have already done the test.
No, it's ok. Are you ready for the questions?
Yes! (Thanks again)
No worries. What's your biggest fear?
To be alone.
What's your superpower?
None. Sorry, jk, being there for people, maybe? But it will depend on who you ask. Maybe listening to people, that's better.
How do you feel when people are not authentic around you?
A bit confused, sometimes it bothers me and other times I wonder why they are this way(how did they get to being this way, or what is their way of being) and if they will change over time to be more themselves, or if this is just the real themselves and they are happy this way.
How do you handle criticism?
Depending on the situations, if it is related to my job or work I take it badly as if my efforts are not enough and I can't do it better cause I am giving everything already and if it is about my personality, well I will take it very badly anyway but I will try to analyze it a lot and try to change it if it's something that affects people in a bad way or just be mad if it's something that people don't accept because of how you are expected to be.
I guess either way criticism makes me feel as if I'm not enough.
How does your ideal partner look?
Tricky one! I guess someone who listens, who accepts me for who I am, who has his own knowledge of things, but also someone who likes to go outside and enjoy life both the big and the little things, someone who likes affection, and talks about things when there is a conflict with an open mind. But I think this would come with me being idealistic too, which means "fixing" issues in myself or accepting them and not living through them.
What motivates you the most?

Being able to do things for myself, to have the freedom and apply the knowledge I have acquired on situation/work and see that things work out, to inspire people to follow their dreams and be helpful.

What type of people do you tend to avoid?

Manipulative people, very authoritative ones or who don't value me I guess.

You seem like an INFP to me.

Example 6:

Hey Sara, I'm one of your followers on YouTube. I read a recent post of yours saying you type people on your Instagram account. I'm pretty sure to be the type I think I am, but I would really love to hear some insight form you if you don't mind. So would it be possible for you to type me? Have a good day!

Hi ☺ Thank you for watching my YouTube channel. What is your type?

I think I'm an INFP!

Have you ever done the test?

Yeah, multiple tests multiple times. Two years ago I started to be into typology. I've always got INFJ. With the last one, I've been getting INFP results.

What feels right to you?

As INFJs are said to be rare, I was wondering if I was really this type. People in my community seemed to debate my type between INFJ and INFP. It made me confused as my mental health wasn't the best either. INFP seems to fit pretty well when it comes to functions, I find other INFPs to be more sensible than me though, but maybe it has to do with the Enneagram and variants.

Your Enneagram is 4?

Yeah, sp/so (the INFPs I find more sensible are 4 sx-dom).

I could ask you some questions if you don't mind?

Sure ☺

Thank you for taking the time to do this.

Don't worry. Tell me what's your biggest fear?

I think it is feeling stuck, hopeless, at a dead-end, realizing I'm not living to my impression I have made the wrong choices in life that I'm not going in the right direction.

How do you feel when you're interrupted?

When I'm interrupted while doing something like studying do you mean?

I don't like my flow to be interrupted, I feel irritated afterward because my focus is lost.

And I need to re-engage myself in whatever I was doing or thinking.

Do you prefer to entertain others or to be entertained?

Hmm, I like to entertain others but only when I feel comfortable with them. It's usually with closer friends/family, children or people I just click with. When I don't feel comfortable, I'm more passive. To answer your question, what I prefer is when we can entertain each other with friends or other people I know. For example, my friend is telling a funny story and I add something funny to it. If I had to choose absolutely between both, it'd be when I entertain others because that means I'm comfortable.

How do you feel when people are not authentic (around you)?

It bothers me, especially when their attitude drifts completely from one situation to another. For example, I was once arguing with my mom. Guests arrive at home and she was all smiling, pretending nothing had happened. I'm less bothered when people are just being polite to soothe disagreements because I do that as well to avoid hard feelings with people who share completely different worldviews than mine.

Would you consider yourself as attention seeker?

I have a weird relation with wanting to be seen versus

wanting to remain hidden. I'm naturally leaning more on the shy side, so getting exposed is a bit too much sometimes. I am a bit uncomfortable when someone puts me in the spotlight too much. At the same time, I like to be recognized for things I'm proud of and I can brag a little bit sometimes. I would say I'm not an attention seeker in the sense that I'm not desperate for people's attention.

I don't try to steal the spotlight, haha.

Do you secretly like jealous partners?

A little bit jealous is fine because it shows in a way that they're worried to lose you and they're attached to you. Too jealous is a turn-off because it screams insecurity and becomes really difficult to deal with. I want my partner to trust me enough in my relations with others.

What is an ideal partner for you?

I'm usually attracted to people who are more assertive than me, but there have been exceptions. I would want someone who can be serious when needed but who can also joke around, someone who understands me and with whom we share some interests in common or who is willing to learn more about each other's interests.

What motivates you the most?

This one is tough haha. I like to reach moments in my life where I feel connected to myself, others and the world. It can be through art or through interactions and through achievements as well. I love to learn about people's experiences and to learn in general.

What do you dislike about people the most?

When they don't want to see their own flaws or incoherence because it's easier to remain ignorant or blame others, and generally people who act in really immature ways.

How does it feel to work with/talk to closed minded people?

It's quite disheartening, like talking to a wall. I am talking here about people who don't really want to see further than what they're already familiar with or what is accepted in a vast majority. It's especially frustrating when it involves topics that concern the well-being of people or the environment.

What harmony means for you?

Inner peace and feeling like on the same wavelength as others around me I think. It's an ephemeral state because disrupts will always happen in life.

Do you struggle with making up your mind?

Yes, especially with tough choices that have important consequences. Less much with more mundane things.

There are some things of which I'm certain, but for the others, it's more difficult.

How do you look at the authorities?

I think they're necessary because otherwise many things would be chaotic, like (good) parenting is necessary to a child to be able to develop into a healthy adult. Or some laws are necessary to regulate society. However, they should be self-reflective about their roles and own structures, constantly revising themselves.

They should use their power wisely.

Thank you for your honest and introspective answers. As a 4 myself, I value that introspection in people. I think that you're an INFJ. ☺

Thank you for your time, Sara! I was really surprised you replied to my first message really fast. Can I ask you why you see INFJ more than INFP?

There are many reasons (your answers) that showed me that you are an INFJ and not an INFP. All of them lead me to an INFJ.

Also, the way you write and the vibe you have are INFJish – I think that your dominant function is observing function.

Your sentences also have Ti manner to them. You are very balanced when it comes to "emotions" and "reasoning".

I never liked my explanations. It's hard to describe...

Thanks, that's fair, like you said I also feel quite balanced between F and T. And yeah, it's hard to articulate thoughts into sentences, I totally understand that.

Well, I will reflect on your answer ☺

Especially dig into Ni-users who are type 4.

You see... This:

"Thanks, that's fair, like you said I also feel quite balanced between F and T. And yeah, it's hard to articulate thoughts into sentences, I totally understand that." – is NiFe.

What could a FiNe have said, haha?

For example, I doubt they would ever say this:

"I think they're necessary because otherwise many things would be chaotic, like (good) parenting is necessary to a child to be able to develop into a healthy adult. Or some laws are necessary to regulate society. However, they should be self-reflective about their roles and own structures, constantly revising themselves."

This is what Fe user who is idealistic would say.

I would say that too.

Alright ☺ Hmm, I'll have a conversation with my friend who I think is an INFP and ask her this question.

Tell me about what happened ☺ *I hope she is not "under your influence".*

Copying your opinions, etc.

She's someone who stays really true to herself (I really admire that in her), so I think she will answer authentically but you're right to think about the influence.

And yeah, I will tell you ☺

I'm not sure what time it is where you live, but I wish you a nice day or evening.

<u>Example 7:</u>

Hi ☺ I've watched a few of your YouTube videos and I really really enjoyed them, I think you are doing a great job making MBTI more and more clear to everyone and easier to understand. I've been reading and watching many videos about that topic but I'm still SO confused. I wouldn't like to tell you what type I think I am but I have a feeling you just know people well enough so you don't even need that… Anyway, what's the way to be typed by you?

Hi ☺ I can type you. Tell me when you're ready.

Wow, so fast, really? I'm ready.

I am typing two people right now so I can do it in one hour. Are you going to be able to do it then?

Yes but perhaps I cannot answer immediately (+/- 5-10 minutes).

No problem.

I'm ready now.

Have you ever done the test?

Yes, a few, but not the official one.

What were your results?

ENFJ. One time INFJ.

Ok. Tell me what's your biggest fear?

Well… A few things-mental illnesses, that my life will turn out meaningless and empty and that I'll not make a difference in this world.

What bothers you more:

1. When people are not living up to your idealized expectations

2. When people are close minded?

2.

Do you often overempatize with people?

I wouldn't say often, but it definitely happened.

Do you prefer to entertain or to be entertained?

It depends on who I am with and depends on the moment another person and my mood but generally, I would choose entertaining others.

Do you feel that most people love you?

I don't think people "love" me literally but the definitely really really like me and have good vibes toward me. It is rather uncommon for someone not to like me personally.

Do you consider yourself as a good person?

Generally, I would say my expectations and standards for myself are too high to say I am good but I am trying really hard to be a good person.

Do you find it stressful when people misunderstand you or don't trust you?

Extremely stressful.

What do you find attractive in a partner?

This may sound strange but depth of intellect, self-confidence and the overall feeling that someone deep down inside has a really good heart and has some kind of inner force, self-confidence.

Also, I am attracted to cold (cold on the outside, soft on the inside), good looking introvert.

Do you like good listeners?

Yes, I do. There is nothing better than a conversation with a person who can REALLY listen ;)

Do you secretly want a jealous partner?

Hmmm, no, not really.

How do you react to criticism?

To be honest... Not very well especially from people I care about but anyone to be 100% honest... People close to me say that sometimes they are afraid to say a word of criticism because they don't want to offend me... and I guess it's true. I try to work on this issue but I have always been like this. For my boyfriend – "you didn't wash dishes very well" is just a sentence, a fact but when I hear that from his mouth I feel personally attacked. I know it sounds silly and immature but this really is my Achilles point :/

Sister, you're an ENFJ.
Welcome to the club ;)
Oh yeah, thank you, Sara. I'm grateful for your time.

<u>Example 8:</u>
Hi Sara☺ I know this is out of the blue and my Instagram is completely bare (I don't have insta and only made it to message you lol) but would it be possible for you to type me? I really trust your instinct and I love all your videos. I've been studying MBTI for four years and I still can't type myself! I even paid a lot of money to be typed by someone else (typed me as ISFP) but I just think it isn't right. If you have time, please put me out of my misery! I can answer any questions you want. Thanks
Sure! I will ask you some questions.
How do you feel about long term planning?
I think long term planning is really important (but not in detail) because I'm scared of kind of being like my dad – waking up and realizing you've been on the wrong journey the whole time. I like to have a vague idea of where I'm going.
Did you ever think of yourself as better than most people?
Not in reality no, but I find myself daydreaming about being the most talented songwriter ever, lol.
Do you feel you are easy going and complicated at the same time?
I definitely am complicated and try to be easy going but I fail, lol. People have described me as cold or boring or serious.
I think you are an ISFP.

<u>Example 9</u>:

Hey Sara. Could you please help type me? I got professionally typed and they said that I'm an INTP but someone argues that I'm obviously an INFJ and I still can't come into a firm conclusion.

Hi ☺ No problem, I can type you. I will ask you some questions. Ready?

Yes, I'm ready!

Ok ☺ cool

What's your biggest fear?

Not being able to achieve my life goal.

How would you describe your energy?

Anxious 40% of the time. People would assume that I'm boring since I look calm and chill on the outside. Not very approachable. But in my best moment, I'm bubbly and goofy.

How do you feel in an environment where you're controlled by others?

I hate it. I don't like taking orders from other people if it's not what I want to do.

Do you feel like you're an independent person?

I'm not financially independent yet, but I consider myself self-sufficient and not needy.

Do you often feel like you need advices?

I like to look for my own advice on the internet and from books. I know what I'm supposed to do but I just don't do it.

Have you ever thought about suicide in your life?

Never. This could be because of my belief about reincarnation and religion (Buddhism). Suicide is never the answer.

How do you feel when you have distress within a close relationship?

It depends on how you define the distress and the type of relationship. If it's something that I can't change or control, I feel frustrated and angry.

Do you mind criticism?

It might hurt a little bit when I get criticized but if it is a reasonable one I can accept it.

Have you ever felt like you don't need people at all?

Yes, I have. There was a time when I didn't have any friends and didn't go out much and I was perfectly fine with it. But then I realized that friends are necessary to be mentally healthy so I'm more social now.

Have you ever been indifferent to the praise or criticism of other people?

Yes, I think so. If I think that I don't deserve the praise I am indifferent towards it. If it's a professional criticism, I can take it.

Have you ever been suspicious of some people?

Not really.

Are you good at "reading" intentions?

Not very good. I think it's because I don't really have much social experience with people.

How do you feel in places with too much noise?

I would get away from them as soon as possible. Stressful and I can't focus.

What about the lights?

I prefer low lighting. Warm lights.

What kind of partner would be ideal for you?

Someone who is intelligent, who can challenge me mentally and who pushes me to grow and be the best I can be. And of course, they have to be supportive and kind as well.

Would you like a jealous partner?

I wouldn't like it. But I want a partner who only looks at me.

What do you mean by that? Possessive partner?

Hmm sort of. But I haven't been in a relationship so I'm not sure if that's what I want.

Do you like to be admired?

No, I don't like being idolized. It feels fake. Because they don't know everything about me and only see the good side.

Have you ever felt like you're helpless?

There was a period when I felt helpless but not anymore.

Are you afraid to be alone?

I like being alone. I don't feel lonely.

Have you ever felt like you're not able to take care of yourself?

Not at all. Maybe when I was younger and immature I felt that way.

How do you feel when your plans are disrupted?

If it's something that I have took a long time to plan and a plan that I looked forward to then I would be angry. But if it's something small, I can improvise it.

Give me an example of that small one.

My friend canceled our meeting to go out for a drink so I asked another friend to go with me instead. I was a little angry but I quickly asked another person.

Are you manipulative?

I am not manipulative if we are talking about unethical action. But if there's something I want to go my way, I would choose the right words the person wants to hear, so I could get the little things I want.

Do you have difficulty expressing disagreement with others because of fear of loss of support or approval?

Yes, I do. But I don't try to go strong in my disagreement but if it's something I feel strongly and if it's worthy of disagreement I would express my disagreement.

Do you often envision the future?

Yes, I think about the future more than I think about the past.

Would you mind someone (partner for example) looking at your phone and messages?

I don't think I would like that, especially if it's done without me knowing.

Do you mind people barging into your space?

I hate it.

Have you ever felt like you're better than most people?

Yeah.

Have you ever felt like people are jealous of you?

I don't think there's anything to be jealous of. My life is not that exciting.

What is your life goal?

My life goal is to use psychology to help people's life. But I'm not going to be a therapist. I want to write a book that can help people.

Are you preoccupied with fantasies about success, brilliance and your beauty?

I don't have any fantasies. Just visions about success and what could be possible.

Do you feel superior to others?

It's both. Sometimes I feel superior and sometimes inferior. My self-esteem is not stable. I want to feel that we are all equal and there is nothing to be superior about.

Are you honest?

Yes.

Do you feel like you are always telling the truth?

80% of the time. If there are things I have to hide I tell lies. Or just not tell them.

Why do you want to help people?

I think that's what we are all supposed to do. Help society.

If you don't give back your life will lack meaning.

How do you feel when you're not having a clear direction?

I feel anxious. Which is what I'm going through right now. When there's no direct clear path, I get worried that I might not be able to do what I want.

Do you have a video of you talking?

What kind of video do you want?

Talking about which topic?

You can say anything. It doesn't have to be long.

-

You are an INTP from what I saw.

I used to see myself as an INFJ for about 2 years. What makes you think I'm an INTP?

Your body language and facial expression. I can tell you're a Ti dom.

Why do you think people come to a different conclusion when typing?

I don't know. I only trust myself.

I trust visual typing more than typing from writing because people can write whatever they want.

I can tell when people are lying. But yes, visual is way easier.

That is a good skill. I can't do that yet. I'm naïve despite being a Ti dom. Do you know why that is?

Because you probably have a different type of intelligence.

I see.

Thank you so much for your time to type me! I really appreciate your work. ☺

I look forward to your future videos as well.

Thank you for being patient. I am glad we have talked.

TYPES IN A FRAME

CONCLUSION

Some understandings and observations are harder to verbalize and systematize, but I strive to work on it. Some things only make sense while they're in my head or while I am observing people. As soon as these concepts are explained, they loses any meaning they once held. Even though not giving the explanations causes me to doubt that I understood the essence of it at all, it is one internal struggle between incomprehension and conviction with doubt and meaninglessness.

I try to get rid of my pride due to my own potential misunderstandings. It is difficult with inferior Ti.

When I think "this man said this sentence for that reason..." it makes perfect sense to me, and I do not need proof in most cases.

Such thoughts provoke reactions when spoken aloud. Most are a thorn in the eye of those who are of a suspicious nature or accept things only when they are realistic, explanatory, or demonstrable. They will often ask me "How do you know", "what if this", "what if that?" Their goal is very often to test the facts and to sharpen their own ego. It is a mental training game for them- a guilty pleasure.

They win me over in a lot of cases because I surrender.

I surrender because I do not see the point in proving what they will never believe, and I also surrender because in order to prove them I would put in a lot of effort, and it is very questionable if it would be successful.

Some of them do not want to understand, they just want to win. Others, however, only want absolute truth and information, but provable by their means in a clear and concise manner. Seeing is believing, and the way in which sight works for them must be predictable and calculated.

When my pride takes over, I think and say: "what if' is a good thing when you do programming, not when you want to know someone's intention".

If I try hard enough, I can explain everything, but I don't see the point, because after an explanation that is inaccurate in many cases, a wave of new questions comes up; arisen from those to whom nothing can be absolute, except for what may possibly coincide with knowledge and methods on by which they base much of themselves. For my occasional pride, the challenges are not so bad. I appreciate the quality ones that make me understand what I wasn't even paying attention to, and that is indeed important. They completely move me out of a safe habitat and take me into deeper places, where I gain more, understand more, and see things more wholly.

Sometimes I think that ratio is overrated. Everything in the world can be explained and proven only if one has the will and a solid logical ability. But is this the essence, the truth?

This world admires a mind. It thinks that this way of observing the world is above all others. That objective reality can be recognized only by thought, reason, and intellect.

The achievements and tremendous momentum of science should not be underestimated. The fact that mind is an important starting point for many useful things, and that it has in some ways made progress, should not be overlooked, but I cannot help but wonder if the current world view is overrated? Is it hiding the essence? The truth?

Are all discoveries and all laws just small tools that facilitate existence, and not the evidence that we are superior compared to the inexplicable?

Is everything actually subjective even when we are sure that it is objective?

Are we small and funny?

Are we playing with importance and knowledge? Can we accept that we do not know and that we will never know?

"Everything flows, everything changes." - Panta Rei.

New worldviews will seem like an absolute in their actuality, and we, for me at least, remain small forever. There is only one thing represented in the linear continuum, if at all, this irreversible sequence exists.